site-specific poems

books by lola lemire tostevin

Site-Specific Poems
The Jasmine Man
Cartouches
Frog Moon
Subject to Criticism: Essays
'sophie
Double Standards
Gyno-text
Color of Her Speech

lola
lemire
tostevin

site-specific poems

The Mercury Press

The publisher gratefully acknowledges the financial assistance of the Canada Council for the
Arts, the Ontario Arts Council, and the Ontario Book Publishing Tax Credit Program. The
publisher further acknowledges the financial support of the Government of Canada through
the Department of Canadian Heritage's Book Publishing Industry Development Program
(BPIDP) for our publishing activities.

Editor: Beverley Daurio
Composition and page design: Beverley Daurio
Cover design: Gordon Robertson

Printed and bound in Canada
Printed on acid-free paper

1 2 3 4 5   08 07 06 05 04

Canadian Cataloguing in Publication Data

Tostevin, Lola Lemire
Site-specific poems / Lola Lemire Tostevin.
ISBN 1-55128-108-2
I. Title.
PS8589.O6758S58 2004   C811'.54   C2004-901681-4

The Mercury Press
Box 672, Station P   Toronto, Ontario   Canada M5S 2Y4
www.themercurypress.ca

for Laurette Lemire

in memory

contents

TILDEN LAKE

Au Nord de North Bay

j'extrais plus de poésie du lac   de la roche
              Robert Dickson

North Magnetic pulls me like a flower
out of the perpendicular
              Phyllis Webb

i

The frozen frame holds
the lake still
   small tilde on the horizon

where a canoe floats
and the air has no weight.

A lure poised over
the visored head of a fish.

   (Any utopian dimension to these images
is solely an ethic of reading. Everything here is dialectical.
The frozen frames contradict the frames that keep moving.)

ii

Images set into motion again.
Like stumbling on a nest sheltering
four speckled eggs for the first time.

Twigs, blades and leaves molded to a bird's
belly pressing against the nest walls. Shaped
and reshaped by each palpitation.

           (Or is it the other way around?)
Does the body adapt to forms around it?
To fossilized shells and bone fragments.
Bits of wood and teeth asleep.

One perfect lithocardite carried deep inside
a pocket. Pulse trapped in stone.

iii

(How did these prairie shots get in here?)

Space is nowhere there. Infinity
always on the move. Towards tilling,
towards harvesting. All that space
in need of extension.

The forest belongs to the past.
To the warp and weft of lichens and mosses.

       (Have you dreamed of a young forest?)

Even dew drops drop full circle in this northern
geometry where the wind cuts corners and carves
a topography of roots laid bare. Twists
them tight as phenomenological observations.

Fifty frogs plus fifty frogs
makes one perfect equation.

iv

Lens scans the scummy pond.
            (Alliteration happens naturally here,
the evergreens everlasting. Cloud–clot.)

Follows an invisible presence
to the island where waves rush.

Tracks loon's long avian bones
as they glide into curve. Baby loon riding
piggyback. A yodel, a slap on water
hoop hoop to the other side.

This must be the intimate immensity
philosophers and poets write about.

Solitude and diffused light.

v

Days when only images speak.

Hardly two words worth hearing except
a scuffling in the brush and the hush
of trout lilies swimming the forest floor.
                    Belly up their yellow bells.

Hardly a sibilant among the warblers
or the black-garbed woodpecker pickaxing
the parchment bark of *bouleau blanc*
bouleau blanc.

                    Except for snake from under
a rock. Red panic in a blink. Shriek!

All night, bulrushes rushing
the stooped moon.

vi

The past takes on a cartoon quality
within these accelerated frames.
Fanciful brackets.
      (Between present and future.)

Two-dimensional slices where space-time's
track follows a child following a caravan
of ants down a garden path. Their prattle
the thoughts of a multitude.

Steady hum.
Parched voice of a crow.
Gilded tunic.
Midas touch.

Over there young Ishmael
eye to eye with a beached walleye.

vii

In this light, blue
is as true as the foliage
of raven's wing.

        Blue makes the mouth water
cold blue in June. Bloodsucker ankles shackled
under the *fauve* green of Elsinore.

        The lake slick and pitch-dark,
never pale cerulean swimming.

Except for a *libellule* lull
moving the very depths.

        (Oh, *barcarole barque.*)

viii

Where the dark lake soughs, marsh
mouth frog, O little dinosaur
its croak an ancient genre.

Throbs and swells in the purple haze
where beaver rears its pompous head
with Thoreau certainty.

        (Tho the lake is not earth's eye
here, the landscape sees itself mainly through the eyes
of a child, where it is destined to become much smaller.)

Another yodel and a slap
delivers the obvious rhyme.

Frog heads for the sun
            legs dangling.

ix

The stone wall built with the determination
of a turtle between the house and the lake. Heroic.
                         (Wall, counsel of resistance
braces itself as snow falls slant and obliterates all forms.)

The house sheds its light, fluent and interfused,
a negative of its summer counterpart.

The lake takes on a concrete meaning.

A reversal of dimension and perspective
as the landscape rewrites itself.

The sudden realization that it hardly
matters if any of this existed.

                         (Exaggeration is the surest sign.
It avoids the unfortunate habit of reduction
caused by seasons.)

x

In rewind, the house perched above
the stone foundation moves in both directions.
Past dwelling a dwelling for the past.

The blank screen glistens. Firefly vigil
or interstellar dust.

The constant here is change.
The constant here is everything stays the same.

Stars collapse. Their luminous shards ride
the waves, scatter their elements: iron, gold,
mercury in the blood. The stuff of generations.

These are not metaphors: we of the north are,
literally, stardust.

ENCRE DE CHINE

(paper as site)

My path was not determined by an artistic gift
but traced through language. Speech is sculpture.
Joseph Beuys

i

The impulse to jot down. Index
finger tracing paths through lampblack
from burning oil and desiccated trunks

of *bouleaux blancs et épinettes*
split into printing blocks.

Wedged-shaped sins of Babylon
baking in the sun. Reeds reaching heaven.
One-hundred-and-fifty feet of waste silk.

Peau de soie.

Leather from the Middle East.
Copper from Burma.

Prayers of Tibetan monks carved
onto smooth bones wrenched
from the shoulders of dead goats.

ii

The ritual of vellum folded into gatherings.
Folding and refolding precise replications
of fat and thin Buddhas.

                                Bee's wings
trapped under translucent wax.

The *Diamond Sutra*. Sixteen-foot scrolls
on the non-existence of things.
                                Bee's wings.

The stationary flit of nothingness.

iii

It's hardly surprising that the goldsmith from Mainz
also invented the printing press. Precious little sticks
held firmly between the fingers. Molten metal poured
into a hinged box for alchemical transformation:

paper for pearls
paper for rubies and gold
paper for armies.

Nor is it surprising that he also invented
the hand-held mirror. Replication at arm's length.

The mirror stage a writing
or vice versa.
                    L'un reflète le reflet de ce que l'autre
a reflété

moveable type.

iv

Heart as site.
                    (A child carrying a lithocardite
deep inside a pocket.)

Not the cabal pounding in the chest
but the *idea* that moves heart and hand.
Perceives itself as perception.
Subdued, molecular.

The immaterial but tangible means
of expressing the subatomic world
of *bouleau blanc et épinette* where words
refuse to seed themselves as landscape.

Grow their own complex architecture.
Les mots a farrago of lines.
                    Paysage dressé au coeur.

v

When science was diffused by *incunabula*.

Latin for *incubator* or *cradle*. Chisel tool
with a serrated edge rocked back and forth
creating a background for knowledge when
knowledge was nomination of the visible.

From his turret in Frauenburg, Copernicus
eyeballs his celestial investigations and inhabits
the universe.
                    (Or is it the other way around? Does
the universe inhabit his turret on the cathedral wall?)

All night, barely aware of the background tick of the book
louse tapping its abdomen against the pages, Copernicus
translates poetry and revises mathematical equations
for fear they could cause cosmological shifts.

vi

*My point with these seven thousand trees was that each would be
a monument, consisting of a living part, the live tree,
changing all the time...*
   Joseph Beuys,
    on planting seven thousand oaks in Kassel

for Kim O.

On the strolling path around Orser Pond,
trees and shrubs planted in memory of writers
and artists who visited Blue Roof Farm, flourish
in spite of bedrock:

a tamarack grove for Greg Curnoe
a golden willow for Matt Cohen

a weeping cypress for Roy Kiyooka
a weeping willow for Roy Kiyooka

a weeping elm for Al Purdy

white pine for Kathleen Milne

English oak for F. R. Scott
a silver spruce for Marion

Russian olives for Cicely

lilacs for Bronwyn Wallace
Japanese cherries for Gwendolyn McEwen

a lilac walk for Jack Chambers
a white birch for Olga

on the edge of the pasture, forming a corner,
two maple rows for Tom Marshall

on both sides of the milkweed monarch garden
sumac for beep,
                    sumac,
                            sumac,
sumac
                        one golden locust.

The question I want to ask: if I‡ were to have
a tree overlooking Orser Pond what would it be?
What rock-bird would nest in my arms?
Enter the sound aspiring to the rustling of leaves.

‡ *The pronoun "I" can be replaced by the reader's name.*

SEMANTIC MEMORY

(monitor as site)

i

At the retirement home where I visit,
the lexical decision time test measures
the speed of word recognition.

Strings of five to seven letters flashed
onto a screen, each string representing
a familiar word or a nonsense combination,
such as *memory* and *momery*
                    (meme, a system of behaviour
passed from mother to daughter).
Memory trace.

The test is repeated with twenty combinations,
the time it takes to recognize each word recorded.

Affection, attachment, love, care, sensibility,
are either too long or too short to qualify.

ii

The semantic decision time task judges
whether a sentence is plausible in the real world:
"The woman fell and broke her hip."

Unlike a line from a poem by Denise Levertov
see me with embryo wings.

Little is understood of a mind
retracing steps, returning to origins.

iii

The incongruity. The cheerfulness
with which these tests are greeted.
Idle chatter.

Sounds pulled by their roots to bridge
unbridgeable distances, so any sound will do.

A sharing and a crossing-through
as mind and eyes try to adjust
to the sensuousness of *senescence*
and *forgetfulness.*

iv

The world lays down a new logic
as words spill out too fast or too late.

Meander invisible lobes, carried along
currents slow as molten metal.
                    (Precious little sticks held
firmly between the fingers.)

In spite of sentences too garbled
to make sense, there is little doubt
you are in a presence too absolute
for words.

v

What is proper here is nothing more
than the impropriety of banality.

Hours staring at a screen.
                    (Firefly vigil
or interstellar dust?)

Enigmatic equations.
But also the satisfaction of knowing
soon the mind will depend on nothing
outside itself. A place without beginning or end.

Time is older here.
And younger.

Only the pulse at the wrist
regulates the clock.

vi

> *What urge will save us now that sex won't?*
> Jenny Holzer

When heart *is* site. Cabal pounding
at the chest as *love* lights up the circuits.

Less so for *eroticism,* the neural network
no longer as tightly strung.
                    (Poetically named, nevertheless,
for it is neither neural nor network.)

The story shifts from its axis and slips
into waves. Stenosis. Software response
modelled on the brain's computing agility
masterminds the script, changes the beat.

Heart as site an image
                    (spurs mind and hand).

vii

The dogged suspicion that words
belong to some other place.
Some other time.

Alien to any country.
To any class or genre.

Alien to this cerebral membrane
on which words suddenly appear.
And disappear.

Cut against the incorporeal hide.

A   PORTRAIT

Le regard du portrait ne regarde rien, et regarde le rien.
Jean-Luc Nancy

i

She had long decided to shun knitting
                    (and phenomenology,)
reality already too loosely knit.

Disposed to waiting, she sat in the garden
for ten days, cautious and wary, and commented
on the flexibility of a dragonfly's tail.

This morning I summoned the dragonfly
and gave it a tail of cabochon chalcedonies
and iridescent wings. Placed it on the flowering
blackthorn in the corner of the garden.

(I considered adding a pearl
but it seemed too baroque.)

ii

The day mother died, my daughter
checked her grandmother's horoscope.
It said it was the day of her unbirthing.

Her death certificate has her cremated
a month before she died.

There was always the desire
for a life lived differently.

iii

She sits in the garden by the purple clematis
where she fell, eating clementines soaked
in *Beaumes de Venise* and speaks in misquotes:

The sense of the world lies within the world,
when it should be: The sense of the world lies
outside the world.

 She is not ready for such leaps.

iv

Her body has turned into a figure of speech. Old
woman yearning to pick up a younger woman's mantle.

Athena on her ray of light laying hands on Peleus's son,
running crooked fingers up and down his unbent spine.

She was never convinced of the just equilibrium
between opposites like youth and old age. Her thin

hair a basket of dried goldenrod, the young
doctor's the black hair of a master race.

v

Old woman's body stripped
of fantasies and blood. Spine
curved into otherness.

Old woman's body
as it slips between orders,
between lip and cup.

Too many words beginning
with their undoing: *disease,
disadvantage, disembodied,
disgrace.*

Language turns on itself. Words
thin as *disposable* tissue.

vi

Eyes penetrating and blue
                  (true as the foliage
of raven's wings) leave everything
to its own device.

A crystal flask of French perfume,
Femme, an offering on the night stand.

The cactus on the sill in full bloom.

I hold her hand long after it stopped
gathering information. Her fingers
knotted by the strain.

Morse codes echoing
the grievance of trees.

                  (*Au nord de North Bay.*)

vii

The world empties.

Harsh lucidity waits to be abstracted
while the heart keeps fluttering
its damned and persistent rumour.

> *L'immortelle est toujours morte.*
> *Sa sécheresse tend à l'éternité.*
> *Son nom grec veut dire: soleil…*

viii

She is taking on the cast of an old photograph,
a woman crossing a road in a mist of rain.

A house on a rock above a lake
made vulnerable by breath.

There is an element to memory
that reaches beyond mere recollection.

A heaviness aspiring to the rustling of leaves.

ix

The clematis where she fell
has withered on its roots.

Ivy spills from the mouth
of the frog by the fence.

An absent woman forfeits all claims.

KEYHOLE SAW

Je suis un arbre qui brûle avec un dur plaisir.
Je suis en train de me faire. Je me fais jusqu'à arriver au noyau.
Clarice Lispector

i

The first time I was introduced to Kiyooka
I heard his name as *keyhole saw* and visualized
the ancient instrument once used to cut keyholes.

With a name like that I figured he was partial
to precision. Details captured through small and framed
points of reference. Glaucous eye to keyhole
better to capture the Pacific rim.

Better to hear the Kyoto airs.

ii

So he must have liked keys, eh?
Musical keys but also those that fit locks
fastened with bolts, clamps and levers
to the tops of old chests. The kind that pulls locks
from their most central point with a clink and a clank
and lots of reverb. *Small birds glancing off windows,*
catching the updraft neath their startled wings.

iii

In an interview, the writer Fred Wah once referred
to "emes," those distinctive units of linguistic
structure, as irreducible units of meaning.
Small constituent cells.

And I was reminded of a film by Charles and Ray Eames,
The Power of Ten, on the relative size of all phenomena
in the universe. The film takes the viewer on an aerial
tour of someone's garden before moving to the outer limits
of the universe, then in successive orders of magnitude
toward the earth until it reaches, say, Roy Kiyooka's yard.

The camera pauses before reaching into the microscopic world
of a pear, revealing its cell walls, its nucleus and DNA,
the subatomic universe of a pear tree.

iv

The last time I saw Kiyooka,
 he asked if he could play his recorder
during a reading I was giving in Vancouver.

Because I was nervous, I said
I didn't think it was such a good idea.
I feared it would throw me.
Pull me from my most central point.

A week later, in Toronto, I received
an extraordinary book of poems,
frogs & others by Kusano Shimpei,
and a note from Kiyooka saying
he particularly liked the segments
I read from a novel I was writing.

v

To this day I feel dreadful
I didn't let him play.

Let his fingers travel the keys,
the high *do*, keynote to his scale.

The boundless stretch of it.

SITE / SEEING

le narcissisme du reflet
le rapport à l'autre en soi
Jean–Luc Nancy

i

It is Easter week in España, the annual
resurrection of braided palm leaves,
votive candles three meters high,
pale lilies tethered to wounded hearts.

Eerie Nazarenes in white robes and hoods
looking like the KKK.
Dead metaphors never laid to rest.

In Madrid, tourists seek redemption in the Prado
and the Sofia. The excitement of seeing *Guernica*
for the first time, its aura reinforced
by every reproduction ever seen.

A function of copies trying to live up to its image.

ii

A haze hangs over Plaza del Carmen
where they burned his writings
and drawings seventy years ago.

The fish-pond in the Generalife Garden
is as long and intricate as his landscape allegories.

A cricket is held prisoner
in the tower of the old castle.

A shudder of cherry trees.

Everything in Granada is Lorca's.

iii

Quisiera saber... I would like to know.

We ask for directions to the Reina Cristina Hotel,
my question drowned out by the rock band
Los Lunes Tormentosos.

The few Spanish words I speak
elicit answers I don't understand.

What language am I *en España?*
Suis-je? Soy?

> *Je veux capter mon <u>est</u>*

Waylaid double with no way
of getting anywhere from there.

iv

We decide on the Reina Cristina
where plants trail from window sills.
Until postcards at the desk inform us this
is where he was hiding when he was arrested.

A marble stairway leads to the rooms
one of which was surely his. Where
he settled into a routine of reading
and playing the piano. Spoke about
his forthcoming collection of sonnets
with Aunt Luisa and his "divine jailer,"
Esperanza.

Light spills in a thin diagonal shaft
from a door left ajar.

We decide against the hotel's three-star
restaurant with rows of white table-cloths.

v

On the outskirts of Granada, drawings pinned
to curtains billow out a window of a summer house.

Jasmine from the damp fields of the *vega*
precipitates a lyrical headache.
I can hardly stay awake.

He wanted to sleep the sleep of apples.

He sleeps instead the sleep of pomegranates,
granadas, while the green green wind sweeps
(and sweeps) the *vega* clean.

vi

> *Barcelona is the colour of a dog running away.*
> Catalan saying

Barcelona is known to abandon tourists behind heavy
iron gates guarded by dragons with stylized talons.

Or plunk them inside a caliph's pavilion with halls
glazed in ox-blood and frame them in sawtooth corbels
and parabolic arches.

Today Miró stands in primary light atop Montjuic.

Picasso's transfigurations of *Las Meninas*
ebb and flow throughout two fifteenth-century
houses on Carrer Montcada. The painter's gaze
fractures perspective and reels the viewer in.

At five in the afternoon,
> *exactly five in the afternoon,*

pigeons whose necks Picasso once wrung
to capture them on canvas have escaped
their lofts in Cannes's *La Californie*
and are fluttering up and down the Ramblas.

vii

The walls of Frank Gehry's museum in Bilbao
are also on holiday. House of the future
dissolves boundaries and integrates elements.

Titanium fish scales glitter *sur les eaux*
of the Nervión, *fuseaux* in the eyes.

Gulls catch their reflections as they fly by.
Limestone blocks have wings.

viii

Wim Wenders's photographs,
Pictures of the Surface of the Earth,
devoid of human beings are, nevertheless,
charged with the *idea* of human presence.

Oldenburg's *Soft Shuttlecock* disguised
as Wim Wenders's angels poised to fall.

Gehry's sharp-edged fish lamps emanate
ghostly apparitions.

Beuys's installations pluck him from his Nazi-youth
and return him as future. Salvaged car.

I walk through Richard Serra's *Snake* of rusty steel,
soft and malleable as skin.

                                  Peau de soie.

I walk through Jenny Holzer's diode aphorisms
cascading from the floor up.

I walk through the legs of Louise Bourgeois's
spider, *Maman,* and out spirals *femme maison.*

Tomorrow I fly home.

ix

Stacks of photographs. Images
reconstituted as reminiscence.

One photograph
of myself taking a photograph.
                    (Replication at arm's length.)

                    Je veux t'écrire comme qui apprend.
                    Je photographie chaque instant.

An act by which I am replaced by a camera,
viewfinder to the eye. *Femme portrait.*

For this is how I come to be.
In looking I see.
                    (A trifling *croquis*.)

x

Á Barbara C.

Drawings prescribed by the size
and shape of the square page.
                    (Dimension determines
the activity within.)

Lines moving in four directions, Theo
van Doesburg's alphabet her theodolite.

All that stacking and packing.
All that rigour of relationships.

Her countercomposition, a happy *moiré*,
keeps readjusting the viewer's
optical references in shadings of black
and not so black, against a white ground.

Where light wells from within.
Holds sway. Traces invisible
through the maze.

Except for one square marked by an X
drawing attention to its performative potential.

Invites the line as future
means of expression.

xi

Alice à la ligne
        (living on the tenth line)

Celle qui réorganize autour d'elle
le concept de l'espace et la distribution
des fleurs. Jardin épistémologique
dans la vallée de sapins.

Lieu doté de bâtiments aussi naturels
que de sculptures taillées de bois et de pierre.

Alice alidade, l'oeil au champs visuel,
bat le contre-temps avec son instrument
de visée invisible. Mesure les angles

de poutres et linteaux,
poulailler au toît circonflexe,
salon au troncs d'arbres
toiles aussi grandes qu'un ciel nord.

Autour d'Alice tout s'offre
comme mirroir au sujet réfléchissant.

Transparence vive qui passe
de l'autre côté de sa blancheur.

JAR DIN

Pour me refaire et te refaire je reviens
à mon état de jardin et ombre, fraîche réalité...
    Clarice Lispector

i

As she sits in her garden, the writer thinks of the verb *to be*
in relation to writing. Must a writer write in order to be?

Or can she sit in her garden on a summer afternoon
and lazily apprehend the world?

Listless, relieved to have come to the end of a project,
all she wants is to experience the larkspur arching
its languorous head, testing the air.

(A line from her novel. Fraudulent.)

ii

She has been invited to contribute to the next issue
of a periodical whose focus will be "work."
The concept of work "as an attempt to embody intention
in a medium where there is always a counterforce."

She has no idea what this means.

Counterforce as in language?
Anyone who writes knows how resistant words can be.

But writing about resistance is precisely what
she doesn't want to do on a summer afternoon.

Doesn't want to write,
doesn't want to think about it
or skirt the issue.

She simply wants to enjoy the state of grace
that follows writing.

iii

The feeling of lightness after months of burrowing
into words. The pleasure of sitting in a garden
watching flowers push skyward from the earth.

The sun is resplendent.
But what else would the sun be?

She sips lemonade and lets herself drift
in and out of empty rest, the cushion
of the chair molding to her body.

Molding herself to a shell like a snail.
The coolness of that image.

iv

She is reminded of rich mandarins who bathed in shells
so large it took two horses hitched to each valve
to force them to yawn in spite of themselves.

Grands bénitiers.

A painting by Bosch, *Shell navigating on water,*
in which ten adults, four children and a dog sit
inside a shell as if posing for a camera.

Larger-than-life distortions of inhabiting.

(Images that gather dreams.)

v

This is the kind of afternoon it is.
What she is thinking when she notices
around her a frantic buzzing. What another
writer once referred to as the *jar din.*

A choreography moving in relation to the sun
to convey to a colony of bees where to find nectar.

Worker bees sucking up sweetness,
storing it inside their bodies, packing
pollen into baskets on their hind legs.

The sound of worker bees as each one orbits its nucleus.
The sound of obsession, the stupid fear of wasting time.

vi

She looks around to locate where the sound
comes from. Whether her garden shelters a hive.

Queen, drone, worker, each one assigned
a place within an order. Each one working
in precision to other bees.

It is the other that teaches each bee
who she is and how to be.

Being-for-others, one philosopher called it.

The writer rests her cheek
against the frosted glass of lemonade.

vii

It is said that the skill with which bees
make and maintain hives surpasses the ability
of masons, carpenters and builders.

Each bee's function programmed,
its instinct intact:

when and how to build honeycombs
when to feed developing bees
when to start a cell in which to raise a queen
when to air condition the hive to keep it cool or warm
when to kill burly, clumsy drones
or sting to death an intruder mouse.

The hive a natural habitat for the function
of inhabiting and being.

viii

One proverb claims that man can build anything
except a hive. Or is it a nest?

The writer is unsure of her facts, her instincts
never as intact as a bee's.

While the bee's work is sufficient to itself
and its order, there exists, at the basis
of the writer's life, uncertainty. Insufficiency.

Always on the lookout for substance
to generate substance.

Like a tick on a branch of that tree.
Inert, waiting for an animal to walk by
so it can drop and dig itself into something vascular.

That's the tick's job.
All it knows and wants to know of the garden
is warm blood.

ix

When out of the blue, a bee traces circuits
around the writer's head before coming
to rest on the arm of the lawn chair.

Removes dirt and pollen from its antennae,
each one twitching, picking up signals, each one
responding to a code.

The bee's movements lethargic and graceful.
Legs, spurs and tongue,
instruments of exploration.
Body covered with hair.

On either side of the head, one compound eye,
made up of a thousand single eyes, moves
in relation to a million infra-things.

Eyes, smaller than the head of a pin, summoned
by the magnified distortions of flowers and trees.

x

Like a compound eye,
               (like a simile)
words distort and magnify.

Yet only in words can the writer apprehend
what buzzes around her and in her head.

Only in words can she see what is being worked,
relevancy consisting only in having been written
whether it captures any essence other than itself.

Words are the natural habitat of inhabiting and being.

xi

The slow secretion as the writer
becomes the person who writes
her body a figure of speech.
                        (Shaped and reshaped
with each palpitation.)

Ritual folding into gatherings.
Shudder of trees.

The warp and weft of lichens and mosses
under the vaulting path for an illusive sun.
                               Cloud-clot.

As the mind moves to the diaphanous
wing-beats of imaginary bees.

                           (The stationary flit of nothingness.)

Acknowledgements

My deep appreciation to the artists and writers mentioned. And to
Beverley Daurio for her editorial acumen.

The uncredited French quotes on pages 25, 49 and 71 are from
Clarice Lispector's *Agua Viva*, as are all other Lispector quotes, trans-
lated from Brazilian by Regina Helena de Oliveira Machado.

The Jenny Holzer aphorism on page 38 comes from "The Survival
Series," displayed on a UNEX electronic signboard. The series, begun
in the '70s, continues to grow and travel the world.

Early versions of some poems have appeared or are about to appear
in *dANDelion, Capilano Review, Tessera, Westcoast Line* and the antholo-
gy, *Experiments in Poetic Daring*, eds, D. Brandt and B. Godard.

My thanks to the Ontario Arts Council for its support.

Author photograph by Jerry Tostevin.

INDIGO

Indigo Books Music & more
Store 280 GST# R897152666
55 Bloor St West at Bay
Toronto ON M4W 1A5
Tel:(416)925-3536 Fax:(416)925-2134

81009 Reg11 ID 275 2:38 pm 24/05/04

Sales for Customer #38200457

S SITE SPECIFIC POE	1 @	15.95	15.95
S 1551281082			
iREWARDS DISCOUNT			-1.60
S RESUME DROWNING	1 @	17.95	17.95
S 1896647944			
iREWARDS DISCOUNT			-1.80
SUBTOTAL			30.50
TAX: GST - 7%			2.14
TOTAL SALES TAX			2.14
TOTAL			32.64
CASH PAYMENT			40.00
CHANGE			7.36

List 33.90 Sell 30.50 Your Savings 3.40